Hurt no living thing:

Ladybird, nor butterfly,
Nor moth with dusty wing,
Nor cricket chirping cheerily,
Nor grasshopper so light of leap,
Nor dancing gnat, nor beetle fat,
Nor harmless worms that creep.

Christina Georgina Rossetti

Bee Inspired: Teaching Resource

Copyright © 2018 by Apiaries & Bees for Communities Inc.

All rights reserved. This book or any portion thereof may not be reproduced or used in any manner whatsoever without the express written permission of the publisher except for the use of brief quotations in a book review.

Printed in the United States of America
First Printing, 2018
ISBN 978-1983636622

Apiaries and Bees for Communities Inc.
23-1941 Uxbridge Drive NW
BOX 63108
Calgary, AB T2N4S5
www.abcbees.ca

Main Contributor: Theresa Romansky
Additional Contributors: Stacey Cedergren, Sara Haney, Jackie Seidel, Eliese Watson
Illustrations: Ricola Fedyna, Katie Romansky
Photos: Apiaries & Bees for Communities, Tracy Crape
Design Coordination: Brandsmith
Design: Valeria Yusim

Acknowledgements

Many of the design and inquiry-based provocations in this resource were designed, in part, by elementary and middle school teachers who joined ABC Bees, along with Jackie Seidel, for an afternoon of hands-on honey bee keeping. Thank you to Katrina Bidulock, Krissie Eberhart, Erin Quinn and Anna Shyleyko-Kostas for their careful reading of an early draft and for their creative curriculum and pedagogical suggestions. Special thanks to Patricia Anderson for her sharp eye and words of wisdom.

"One can no more approach people without love than one can approach bees without care. Such is the quality of bees…" Leo Tolstoy

What is a book that speaks of bees that does not also speak of people? When I started Apiaries and Bees for Communities (ABC Bees), it was with a small intention: to learn how to keep bees and to make friends. As time has passed, the intention has remained the same, but the projects, opportunities, and connections have changed in scale. We grow as the hive mind grows, with ignited passions for education, youth, and support for life-long learning.

This book is a representation of that passion and collaboration within a group of women who understand the beauty and importance of pollinators. Bees aid in communicating difficult topics of societal functions, environmentalism, mutualism, success and collapse. Putting bee behaviours and communal characteristics under a lens allows for deep reflection on the inner workings of human behaviour, decision making, and intentions. Critical thinking, in my opinion, is the greatest skill that can be taught.

In offering hands-on beekeeping opportunities to over a thousand children and adults through the years, we are reminded over and over again of one thing: that awe and wonderment follow the bees. I invite you to join us and bring the wonderment of bees to your classroom. And with this new knowledge, I challenge you to ask questions about the way things are, dare to dream of something better, and inspire courage to make it so.

"Let us remember: One book, one pen, one child, and one teacher can change the world." Malala Yousafzai

Welcome,

Eliese Watson
Founder
Apiaries and Bees for Communities

FOREWARD

Dear Teaching Colleagues,

I am honoured to write this introduction and invitation to this exceptional teaching and learning resource. Deciding to learn about bees with our students may be one of the most life-changing decisions we could make as educators. As we learn collaboratively with our students, we can aim to cultivate curiosity about bees and about our complex and interdependent relationship with them.

Bee Inspired... The word *inspired* in the title of this resource matters, and also holds an important double meaning. Derived from Latin, the English word inspire originally referred to breath or breathing, and to spirit or to breathe life into something (we can still hear the connection to *respiration*). To *Bee Inspired* implies remembering the even deeper relations bees have in interdependent, ecological life cycles. All living beings share the same planetary breath.

This resource is designed as a curriculum support for elementary and middle school teachers (K-8). It describes the best and latest scientific understandings about bees in a concise and organized way that will support teachers in developing expertise and an essential grounding in the topic. Throughout the resource are sections called "Opportunities for Inquiry". These inquiry-based provocations encourage us to go far beyond learning 'facts' such as the parts of an insect body, or their life cycles. They remind us to pay attention to designing holistic, interdisciplinary learning experiences that focus on the entire ecological systems that support the life of bees. Some of these might take a short time, while others might lead to a whole year's inquiry with lasting community actions.

As a teacher, you will know which provocations might be most appropriate and likely to *inspire* your learners. No doubt, as you learn together, the students' curiosity will naturally raise many more questions. Follow these.

The purpose of learning about bees is not to "save the bees". Rather, it is through learning about bees that we may become concerned and knowledgeable, not only about bee life cycles, behaviors, and habitats, but also about what sustains our human lives and our communities.

When we learn about bees, we also learn about ourselves. It is this vision that undergirds all of ABC Bees' work including this teaching resource. Thus, learning about bees, if done in the spirit of learning together in wonder and awe, has the potential to affect the wellbeing and health of your classroom community, your school community, and the wider human and non-human community on the planet.

One of the most inspiring statements in this resource is:

It is not necessary to keep a hive or have acres of land to make an impact. Simple changes to one's own patch of green creates a stitch, that when replicated, can begin to weave nature back through communities.

If you have been searching for a perfect resource to accompany you while teaching and learning about bees in your classroom, this is it!

Bee inspired. Remember to breathe. Enjoy your learning.

Jackie Seidel
Associate Professor, Curriculum and Learning
Werklund School of Education

PREFACE

I would like to express tremendous gratitude to Eliese Watson for her warm friendship, expertise and unwavering support. Several years ago, eager to learn more about bees I took her Level One Beekeeping course and fell deeply in love with the sweet honey bee.

From there it was a hop, skip and jump back to my kindergarten classroom to share with them what I had learned. Children call me back to the magical world of animals; and Christina Rossetti's poem: "Hurt No Living Thing," has provided an impetus throughout my teaching career by introducing the importance of small creatures that cannot protect themselves.

As the weeks turned in to months, the children in my classroom and I eagerly explored and celebrated these amazing pollinators, and this is when the concept for this book was created. After five years of labor, research, and love, here you have it in your hands.

A special thank you to the many people who enthusiastically sustained the undertaking of this project; here in Alberta, British Columbia, Ontario and the Netherlands. To the children who shared their creative drawings and inspiration, for the drawings by my talented daughter Katie, and my beekeeping mentor John Armstrong for guiding my hands-on learning of honeybees. Thank you to countless others - colleagues, beekeepers, dear friends and family - YOU are all champions of the bee!

Thank you to my partner Gene for your love, support and belief in this project from its inception.

My sincere wish is that you all enjoy discovering the beauty and brilliance of the bee. May we all celebrate our gratitude and respect in some small measure by taking responsibility for restoring and protecting their well-being.

In gratitude,
Theresa Romansky

TABLE OF CONTENTS

1. WHAT IS A BEE 2
   1.1 Bee Classification 2
      1.1.1 What's in a Name?
   1.2 Anatomy of Bees 3
      1.2.1 Body Regions
      1.2.2 Body Parts & Function
   1.3 Identifying Bees vs. Other Insects 13
   1.4 Types of Bees 15

2. BEES IN THE ENVIRONMENT 18
   2.1 Plants and Bees 18
   2.2 Nesting Sites 21
   2.3 Predators and Defense 24

3. BEES AT HOME 26
   3.1 Members of the Hive 27
      3.1.1 Honey Bee Colonies
   3.2 The Birds and the Bees 31
      3.2.1 Solitary Bees
      3.2.2 Social Bees
      3.2.3 Swarming
   3.3 Hive Products 37
      3.3.1 Honey
      3.3.2 Pollen
      3.3.3 Propolis
      3.3.4 Royal Jelly
      3.3.5 Beeswax
   3.4 Honey Bee Communication 41
      3.4.1 The Waggle Dance
      3.4.2 Pheromones

4. BEES AND PEOPLE 44
   4.1 Honey Bee Management 44
   4.2 Supporting Local Bees 46
      4.2.1 Food
      4.2.2 Nesting Sites

5. GLOSSARY 50

6. REFERENCES 56

1. WHAT IS A BEE

1.1 Bee Classification

All organisms are categorized according to their taxonomic rank, which groups species according to similarities and provides detailed descriptions of organisms at a species level. Descending from most general to most specific, the categories are kingdom, phylum, class, order, family, genus, species.

All bees belong to the phylum, Arthropoda, which is characterized by the presence of a protective exoskeleton, paired jointed legs and segmented body. Animals in this phylum are also invertebrates, meaning they have no spine.

Bees are further divided into the class Insecta due to the presence of three pairs of jointed legs, three body segments (head, thorax and abdomen), a pair of antennae and compound eyes.

Bees, as well as wasp and ants, belong to the order called Hymenoptera which means "membranous or transparent wings". Other insects, like grasshoppers, have leathery wings while butterflies are characterized as scaly. Insects in Hymenoptera go through complete metamorphosis and usually have two pair of wings, though they're not always present in all life stages.

Bees are then further broken down into seven family groups and numerous genera (plural for genus) and species. The number of bee species worldwide is thought to be over 20,000.

Opportunities for Inquiry:

Most taxonomic names have their roots in Latin, which often provides literal descriptions of the species' characteristics. The honey bee, *Apis mellifera*, translates to "bee" and "honey-bearing".

- Investigate other names in the bee or animal world.
- How does the taxonomic name help describe the species they represent? For example, *Triceratops* translates to three-horned face.
- Do some of these words provide roots for words in other languages?

1.1.1 What's in a Name?

The Merriam-Webster's Dictionary spells 'honeybee' as one word but according to entomologists the spelling is two words, 'honey bee', because a honey bee is an insect classified as a bee. Likewise, bumble bee and mason bee are also two words.

When in doubt, there is a short rhyme that one can use as a benchmark for the spelling of an insect's name: "If true, then two".

A house fly and a robber fly are taxonomically classified as flies. Conversely, dragonflies and ladybugs are not classified as flies or bugs, therefore their names are run together.

1.2. Anatomy of Bees

1.2.1 Body Regions

Unlike humans, whose skeleton is inside and allows room for the body to grow, bees have an exoskeleton. This tough exterior is made from small, movable plates of chitin which prevents the body from growing, provides some protection from predators and protects bees from dehydrating.

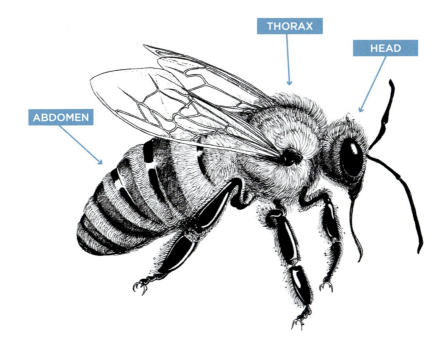

1. WHAT IS A BEE

Head - Used in sensing the environment and for feeding. There are two large compound eyes, three small simple eyes, two antennae, a tongue and mouth parts.

Thorax - Aids in transportation of the bee. There are six legs, four wings and muscles for movement.

Did you know?

A honey bee weighs as much as four to five grains of dried rice.

Abdomen - The abdomen contains the majority of the respiratory, circulatory, digestive and reproductive organs. The stinging apparatus is also located in the abdomen.

1.2.2 Body Parts & Function

Antennae

- Bees have two antennae located on their head that are covered in tiny hairs and approximately 3,000 sensory organs.

- Bees spend a large amount of time in a dark hive so they need to use their antennae for taste, smell, touch and even hearing, to communicate with each other.

- Bees have 170 odour receptors, giving them a complex sense of smell, vital for detecting nectar, pollen, water, tree resin, smoke, predators and alert pheromones from other bees. Their sense of smell is about 100 times more sensitive than that of a human.

- Bees have two hearing organs that are membranes on their antennae, another similar set is on their legs. They do not hear airborne sounds using a tympanic organ (ie. eardrum) like we do, but they can detect vibrations from other bees which are converted to nerve impulses. The hair-like structures that detect these vibrations are also sensitive enough to respond to oscillations in air particles created from sound waves.

Opportunities for Inquiry:

- What do a dolphin's melon, a bee's antennae and a snake's jaw have in common?
- Explore how other animals 'hear' and the physiological features they have to help them.
- What are examples of this technology in the human world?

Compound Eyes

- Bees have two large compound eyes located on either side of their head, made up of almost 7,000 individual hexagonal units known as ommatidia, each with a single lens that receives visual signals.

- Honey bees can perceive movements that are separated by 1/300th of a second while humans can only sense movements separated by 1/50th of a second. This precision allows bees to see the world quite differently. If a bee were watching a movie in the theatre it would be able to see each individual frame being projected, similar to how we see an animation flip book.

- The compound eyes gather information about distance, colour and flickering light.

- The tiny hairs around the bee's eyes can detect the direction and speed of the wind which aids in flight.

- The drone's eyes are bigger so they can see and track queens more effectively on mating flights.

- The queen spends most of her life in the darkness of the hive so her eyes are smaller than those of the worker bees.

Did you know?

A bee has so many eyes and such sensitive sight that rapid movements made by us are alarming and extremely exaggerated. That's why it is best not to swat at a bee!

1. WHAT IS A BEE

- Bees see a range of light wavelengths that is slightly shifted from our visible range. Bees are unable to see the colour red, but can detect ultraviolet wavelengths that are invisible to us.

- A flower that looks orange to us (red light combined with yellow) might look dark green or black to the bees.

- Many flowers have ultraviolet patterns on them that help guide the bees to the flower's nectar. They often resemble bull's eye or landing strip patterns.

Opportunities for Inquiry:

- How does a bee's vision compare to the way other insects, animals or humans see colour?
- What would a bee's painting of their world look like, without the colour red?

Simple Eyes

- Bees have three simple eyes, called ocelli. They are set in a triangular shape on the forehead in-between the two compound eyes.

- These eyes do not see images like our eyes do. They sense patterns and intensity of light and darkness.

- The primary purpose of simple eyes is to track the sun's light and intensity for navigational purposes. Bees can detect polarized light and can see the sun even when it is hidden by the clouds.

Did you know?

Beekeepers wear white clothing because bees tend not to land on white but do have a defensive instinct towards dark colours, which resemble large predators.

Mouth

- A bee's mouth is located on the head. It consists of an upper and lower jaw which contain mandibles, tooth-like appendages that are used to chew pollen, cut leaf pieces and mold wax.

Glossa

- A bee's hairy, long tongue is called a glossa and is located within a protective sheath, made up of more rigid maxilla and palp. The three parts are collectively called the proboscis. When not in use, it is tucked under the mouth.

- The glossa is stretchy like a human tongue, works much like a straw and is used to suck up nectar, honey and water.

- The young bees assigned to take care of the queen bee use their hairy tongue to lick her body clean.

- The tongue length of a bee varies significantly between species and is closely connected to the type of flowers the bees prefer to forage.

Brain

- The honey bee brain is small, about the size of a sesame seed, though it is more dense than a human's brain.

- Social bees have bigger brains for learning and memory than do solitary bees.

- As bees age, their memory fades and the ability to learn decreases. Research studies have also shown that, like humans, not getting enough sleep will impair a honey bee's communication skills.

1. WHAT IS A BEE

Wings

- Bees have four wings attached to the thorax, two large forewings and two smaller hindwings. The back wings hook together with the front wings, like a Velcro seal, for flight and unhook when the wings are folded and not in use.

- The two pairs of membranous wings have low air resistance and allow the bee to fly forward, backward and sideways.

- The primary use for the bee's wings is flight, allowing the bees to travel, find food and escape danger. However, bees can also use their wings for temperature control; fanning their wings to cool the air. They'll often use water combined with fanning in the hive to create air conditioning effects.

- Honey bees are also able to disengage the wing muscles from their wings, allowing them to vibrate without moving. These vibrations are used to generate heat.

- Bumble bees use a similar technique to stay warm on cool days and are able to pollinate at lower temperatures as a result.

> ### Opportunities for Inquiry:
> A prevailing myth states that bumble bee flight is aerodynamically impossible. Recent science has proven otherwise, relating bumble bee flight to that of helicopters. Examine how different animals fly, or glide, through the air. Consider bees, butterflies, bats, birds, or even squirrels!
> - How are their wings the same or different?

- Bees are not particularly fast fliers, averaging about 24km/hr. Dragonflies are considered some of the fastest insects, reaching speeds of up to 56km/hr.

- During flight, the honey bee maintains a body temperature of about 35 degrees Celsius by cooling herself off with regurgitated droplets of watered-down nectar, just as mammals use sweat to cool their bodies off.

Did you know?

The buzzing sound a bee makes comes from beating their wings approximately 180 times a second. Many animals, including humans, may interpret the buzzing as a first warning that a stinging insect is nearby. However, buzzing is more often a by-product of other activities or, in the case of honey bees, a complex form of communication.

Legs

- Bees have six jointed legs, with three located on each side of the thorax. They use their legs for walking, prying flowers open, gathering and carrying pollen, communication, cleaning themselves and their fellow bees and detecting oxygen levels and temperature.

- Bees have claw-like tarsi (feet) with suction cups at the bottom of each leg which help them to hang onto rough surfaces and climb vertical surfaces.

- Also in the region of the tarsi is the tarsal gland which is responsible for footprint pheromones in honey bees, assisting them in the search for nectar.

- Bees also have a set of hearing organs on their legs.

- In many species, the legs of females have hairs adapted to holding pollen. The bee uses her front legs to brush the pollen off and pack it onto the back legs which have pollen baskets or pollen brushes.

1. WHAT IS A BEE

Did you know?

Honey bees exhibit a unique behavior called festooning, where dozens of bees will cling together to form a chain-like fabric hanging from combs or in between two sheets of comb. The exact reason for this behavior is unknown, though it is thought to be related to wax building and is often used as a sign that there is a queen in the colony.

Pollen Baskets

- Female honey bees and bumble bees have pollen collecting structures on their legs called corbicula or pollen baskets. The corbicula are composed of stiff hairs into which the bees pack compressed pollen moistened with nectar and bee secretions.

- When the baskets are empty they are shiny, and when they are full of pollen they range in colour from deep yellow to a reddish colour, depending on what the bees have collected.

- Other species of bees use scopae or pollen brushes to store smaller quantities of dry pollen. These hairs are located on the legs or the underside of the abdomen, depending on the species.

Spiracles

- Along the length of the abdomen, bees have small, circular openings in their exoskeleton called spiracles which allow them to breathe.

- Spiracles are openings to a network of air sacs and tracheas that allow bees to take in oxygen and release carbon dioxide, like human lungs.

Hair

Bees are covered with fuzzy, branched hairs which collect pollen and help regulate body temperature.

As the bee flies through the air, the friction generated with her hair builds up a positive electric charge (similar to rubbing a balloon on one's head or arms). When she lands on a flower, which is grounded and therefor negatively charged, the pollen is attracted to the positive charge and sticks to the bee as she shakes the pollen loose.

As the bee continues foraging, loose pollen that has not been packed into the corbicula or scopae is transferred to the next flower, completing the pollination process.

Stomach

- All bees have a primary stomach as part of their digestive system, but some bees also have an additional 'stomach' or thin-walled, expandable, sac-like structure called a honey crop.

- The honey crop is a short-term storage place for water or nectar and is not part of the bee's digestive tract. It contains special enzymes that start the fermentation process in the honey.

- Bees make honey mainly from the nectar of flowers but traces of honeydew (made by aphids), plant sap and pollen can also be found.

Stinger

- Only female bees have stingers, which are located at the very end of their abdomen.

- Early in the evolutionary branching from wasps to bees, the purpose of the sting was to paralyze insect prey to be fed to offspring. As bees evolved away from meat-eating, their sting became a defensive function.

- Female honey bees have barbed stingers. When they sting an animal with tough skin, like a human, their stinger gets pulled out of their body along with the part of their digestive track, causing them to die.

1. WHAT IS A BEE

- Most bees have a smooth stinger and can sting repeatedly, however many of the smaller solitary species do not have a stinger that is strong enough to penetrate human skin. Furthermore, solitary bees do not have a colony or honey to defend, so are much less likely to behave defensively around their nests.

- Stingless honey bees do not sting. Instead they bite, leaving saliva that irritates and burns the skin. These bees are only found in tropical and subtropical regions.

Did you know?

Bees are vegetarians —they get all their required nutrients from pollen and nectar. Because they are not hunters or scavengers, they are not aggressive when seeking out food and will only sting if provoked or harmed.

1.3 Identifying Bees vs. Other Insects

The common perception of a bee is a flying bug with distinct black and yellow stripes on its abdomen. However, this image can lead to a frequent misidentification when encountering insects. Many wasps and flies can have black and yellow markings while most bees are actually quite dull in colour with more subtle patterns. To distinguish between these insects, there are a few key characteristics to keep in mind.

Wasps

- Wasps, which include hornets and yellow jackets, are carnivores and scavengers. Though they may visit flowers for a sip of nectar, this is not their main food source and they do not collect pollen. If an insect is investigating a hamburger at a picnic it is most likely a wasp.

- Tend to be more brightly coloured with noticeable patterns.

- Generally appear hairless, as they do not need to attract or hold pollen. This can make the 'waist' (between thorax and abdomen) appear thinner.

- Social wasps are the most commonly encountered species, though there are many, less aggressive, solitary species. All can be beneficial for controlling insect pest populations.

- Paper wasps create the familiar grey-brown paper nests that can be found hanging from trees or roofs. Bees never create nests like these.

1. WHAT IS A BEE

Flies

- Generally only have a bit of hair on their thorax and do not carry pollen.

- Can be dull in colour or have noticeable stripes on their abdomen.

- Have only two wings, instead of four.

- The easiest way to differentiate between a fly and a bee is to look at the head. Flies have large eyes that occupy the bulk of the head and almost touch at the top. Their antennae are much shorter than a bee's.

Did you know?

There are a few species of bees known as cuckoo bees, similar to a cuckoo bird. They lay their eggs in the nests of other bees who will care for their young. Because these females do not provision their own nests, they do not carry pollen. Their lack of pollen-carrying hairs makes them easier to confuse with wasps.

Opportunities for Inquiry:

Practice observing and identifying bees and other insects outside in your neighbourhood or by using photos.

- What types of plants are they found on or attracted to? What is your evidence?

- What features helped to identify the insect? Pay particular attention near blooming plants on sunny days as these will be visited by many different bees and other pollinators.

1.4 Types of Bees

Over millions of years, bees have adapted to Earth's diverse and ever-changing ecosystems, from scorching deserts, to lush rainforests and cool alpine meadows, where there are flowers, bees have found a way to survive. Some live in a range of climates while others are suited to very specific environmental conditions. Each type of bee has a certain lifecycle, nesting habits, and foraging needs. Knowing a little about the bees in a given area can help one to determine the best ways to provide supportive habitats.

Though some bees are easy to spot, like the familiar bumble bee, others, like the 2mm long *Perdita* are easy to miss. Unlike large mammals or birds, identifying bees at the species level can be rather difficult. Most bee enthusiasts will aim to narrow down the genus to which a bee belongs instead. Understanding a few key characteristics can help to narrow down the options and, after a little practice, identification can become a fun treasure hunt.

Did you know?

There are over 20,000 different species of bees and they can be found on every continent, except Antarctica.

Below are a few common genera of bees and some tips for identifying them in the wild. Most bees are named for a distinctive physical feature or behavioral habit. Remember, the scientific convention is that the name of the genus is always capitalized, while the species is not. Both are italicized or underlined.

Apis mellifera - Latin for "carrier of sweetness", the honey bee, this social bee is not native to North America but was brought to the continent with early settlers and is now commonly found throughout the continent.

- About 1-1.5cm long, with a fuzzy thorax and subtle abdominal stripes. Females carry clumps of pollen in corbicula on their hind legs.

15

1. WHAT IS A BEE

Bombus sp. - Bumble bees are 1-2.5cm long, are quite fuzzy and have distinct, colourful hair patterns that can be used to identify bees at the species level.

- Females carry clumps of pollen in corbicula on their hind legs.
- From the same family as honey bees; also live in colonies and use wax to make their nests.

Opportunities for Inquiry:

Bumble bees can be identified at the species level using their colourful hair patterns.

- Observe and record (draw, paint, photograph, etc.) the pattern of bumble bees spotted outside and compare with species guides in books or online. Most areas are home to several different species. A few examples include:

Andrena sp.- Known as miner bees, 0.5-1.5cm long, named for their underground nesting habits.

- Can be black, blue or green with subtle stripes on their abdomen
- Females carry pollen in scopae on their hind legs

Lasioglossum sp. - 0.5-1cm long, known as sweat bees because they are attracted to salt in mammal sweat.

- Usually black, but can be metallic blue or green with a striped abdomen
- Females carry pollen along their hind legs

Hoplitis sp. - Use mud to build their nests giving them the name mason bee

- 0.5-1.5cm long, most are black, though some can have red abdomens
- females carry pollen on the underside of their abdomen

Megachile sp. - Called leafcutter bees because they use leaves to line their nests

- 1-2cm long, with stout bodies and upturned abdomens usually dull in colour
- carry pollen on the underside of their abdomen

Opportunities for Inquiry:

As a class, or in groups, design observation keys to help others living in your neighbourhood to identify local bees.

- **Explore different logic tools to decide which would be most useful (decision flow charts, plant-id keys, etc.).**

2. BEES IN THE ENVIRONMENT

In their native ecosystems, bees play a key role amongst their community of living organisms. Indeed, bees (along with other pollinators) are often considered keystone species, without whose presence their ecosystem would change dramatically. Bees are also reliant on living and non-living components of their ecosystem to provide a ready source of food, water and nesting areas.

2.1 Plants and Bees

The mutualistic relationship between plants and pollinators creates the foundation on which most ecosystems thrive. Healthy plant life ensures a food source for many animals, microorganisms in soil, shelter, soil stability and other benefits. Without bees and other pollinators this support system crumbles.

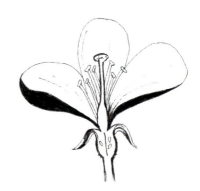

Pollination is the reproductive fertilization of a plant and occurs when pollen from the anthers of one flower is transferred to the stigma of another flower. The grain of pollen, containing its genetic material, travels down the pistil to the ovule where it triggers seed production.

If plants are not properly pollinated, they are unable to produce healthy seeds. This impacts both the quality of a crop (ie. poor tasting fruits) and the health of a plant population (ie. fewer healthy offspring resulting in low overall population resiliency).

Some plants can self-pollinate, but most require cross-pollination; the movement of pollen between two different flowers or individual plants. For many grasses, trees and cereal crops, wind is the mechanism for cross-pollination, but for more than two-thirds of plants, an animal is required to move the pollen. There are numerous bats, birds and insects that offer pollination services, but bees are generally considered to be the most effective.

Opportunities for Inquiry:

Humans also rely on pollination for food production. Design a way to record and study the various ingredients in your lunches or snacks to explore different forms of pollination.

- What plants are part of the meal and how are they pollinated?
- If animal products are in the meal, what types of food do the animals eat that may have required pollination?

Plants entice bees to pollinate them by providing two nutritious sources of food; pollen and nectar. The nectar provides carbohydrates and the pollen contains protein, amino acids and other nutrients – all the food a bee needs to survive.

The colour, size, shape, odour and bloom time of a plant determines which kind of pollinators it will attract and act as cues to let bees know when they are ready to be pollinated. As bees are foraging, they are attracted to colourful, scented flowers and their ultraviolet markings, which direct bees to the pollen and nectar.

The honey bee has hair-like structures in its mouth, antennae and the tarsi of their front legs which detect sugary tastes. When the worker bee lands on a flower it will immediately extend its tongue if it detects a sweet nectar taste from its tarsi.

2. BEES IN THE ENVIRONMENT

> **Opportunities for Inquiry:**
> Take an observing walk noting the different kinds of flowers nearby. Record their shapes, colours and any visitors.
> - Can the reproductive structures of the flower be seen?
> - How are they the same or different from other flowers?
> - Would these flowers be easy or difficult to pollinate?

When the pollination process is complete, the flower slows its production of nectar and attractive scents and may also change colour or wilt. Scientists have discovered that bees will also use pheromone signals to avoid flowers that have recently been visited by another bee and now have depleted nectar or pollen. Bee scientist and researcher Dave Goulson describes this: "When a bee lands on a flower petal, it leaves behind a smelly footprint which alerts other bees that the flower has recently been drank from. Each bee species and other flying insects as well, have their own unique footprint smell."

Did you know?

Millions of years ago the appearance of bee fossils occurred relatively at the same time as the arrival of flowering plants on which the bees fed and pollinated.

Specialization:

Bees and flowers evolved alongside each other, developing physical features that complement one another and, in some cases, a particular preference between certain species. Adaptations that impact plant choice can include body shape and size, length of the tongue and the behavior. Bees that only forage on a specific type of flower, like those in the genus *Dieunomia*, are known as oligolectic, or simply, specialists. Bees that forage on a range of plants, like those in the genus *Bombus*, are called generalists.

Ecosystems with specialist plant-bee relationships can be vulnerable to environmental changes, especially if they are somewhat isolated. If an ecosystem becomes inhospitable to a certain specialist bee species due to climate change or development, it can cause a subsequent decline in the corresponding pant species, potentially creating a domino effect through the entire ecosystem.

2.2 Nesting Sites

Another key habitat requirement for bees is a suitable nesting site. Like most animals, bees need a safe space to house their offspring. The most recognizable bee nest is the honey bee hive, filled with sheets of wax comb and busy worker bees. However, most bee species have much more modest nests that are often imperceptible to the casual observer.

The majority of native bees in North America are ground-nesting. They either seek out existing burrows, made by rodents or other insects, or dig out tunnels in bare or sparsely vegetated soil. Underground nests can be found in almost any habitat, from the slopes of stream beds to sandy deserts, each species has their preference, related to what is available within their native range.

The remaining species of bees are predominantly wood-nesting. These bees will seek out existing holes or crevices in trees (made by other insects) or seek out woody plant stalks (ex. raspberry canes) and tunnel into their soft, pithy centers.

Whether ground or wood-nesting, bees often use other materials, like mud, leaves, petals or masticated plant matter, to protect their nest from moisture, disease or predators.

Opportunities for Inquiry:

Research the kinds of homes bees build. Experiment with different nest building materials to make a sculpture or imitation bee home.

- Are the materials easy to work with? Easy to find?
- What properties make them useful for a bee building a home?

2. BEES IN THE ENVIRONMENT

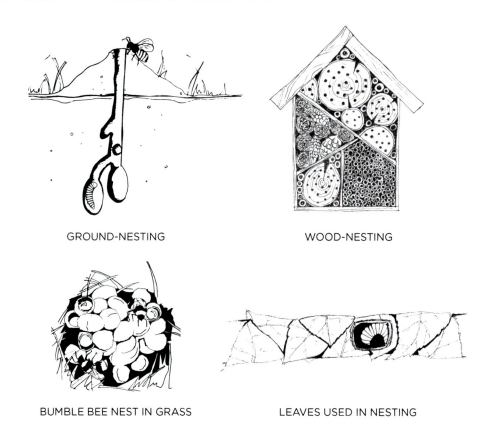

GROUND-NESTING

WOOD-NESTING

BUMBLE BEE NEST IN GRASS

LEAVES USED IN NESTING

Though bees are specially adapted to carry pollen as they fly to and from their nest, there are some limitations to their foraging range. The distance a bee can fly is closely related to her size. The smaller the bee, the shorter the distance she can travel.

Some solitary bees are only able to fly as far as 150m, while honey bees and bumble bees can travel great distances, up to 20km in some cases, though these bees typically have flights in the 1-5km range. It is important that floral resources are located within the flight range of the bee's nest as increased distances cause decreases in nest productivity.

Did you know?

Some species of bees have special glands that produce a cellophane-like substance which they use to line their nests to keep moisture out.

Opportunities for Inquiry:

A bee's habitat range and choice of nest location is closely connected to their habitat needs. Similarly, people usually plan their homes, communities or cities around proximity to resources. Investigate and explore what makes a good environment for a bee, other animal, or person.

- What are the similarities or differences?
- How would one demonstrate these needs (map, web, etc.)?

Bees, like most other living organisms, also require a source of water for survival. For most bees, shallow puddles of water or dew will do the trick. For honey bees though, a steadier supply is necessary as it is needed for maintaining hive moisture level, temperature control (air-conditioning), and feeding larvae. It is not uncommon to find groups of honey bees visiting bird baths or paddling pools to collect water for the hive.

2. BEES IN THE ENVIRONMENT

2.3 Predators and Defense

Beyond pollination, bees serve a secondary role in ecosystems as well: as a food source for animals further up the food chain. Some birds, toads and insects will hunt adult bees while they are foraging, but the majority of predators will seek out larvae to feed on.

Birds, hornets and wasps are known to raid the nests of ground or wood nesting bees. Honey bee hives and bumble bee nests are vulnerable to larger predators like skunks, badgers and bears, who happily gorge themselves of a combination of stored nectar, pollen and larvae.

Bees can be vulnerable to smaller organisms as well. Mites and other parasites can feed on young bees and spread diseases throughout populations. The varroa mite is one of the most familiar threats due to its prevalence in honey bee colonies. This is a tiny, reddish brown, spider-like animal about the size of a pin head. The Varroa mite and its offspring feed off the blood of bees in the larval or pupae stage. This weakens the bee's immune system and can cause deformed body parts as well.

The bee's primary defence is its stinger, which may be used to defend nests or ward off attacks from predators while foraging. For much of their evolutionary history the bee's primary predator has been other insects. As a result, the stingers on most bees are able to easily penetrate insect exoskeletons but are usually not strong enough to penetrate the skin of humans or other mammals. Bees with larger colonies, like bumble bees or honey bees, are a more common target for larger predators and therefore have stronger stingers.

Unlike the honey bee, native bees in North America do not leave their stinger behind when they sting. Even though the act of stinging does not kill the bee, attacks are risky, so most solitary species have adapted to avoid predators rather than defend their nests. Furthermore, most bees are encountered while they are busy foraging and will therefore only attempt to sting if they are trapped or handled roughly.

When a honey bee stings, it curls its body so that it can actively push its barbed stinger into its attacker. The venom sac pumps in venom creating a sharp pain with possible tissue swelling. When the honey bee flies away, the barbed stinger, venom sac and lower digestive tract remain stuck in the skin of the attacker and the bee soon dies as a result.

Did you know?

Only female bees have stingers which are thought to have evolved from their reproductive system.

Opportunities for Inquiry:

Take a noticing walk in your neighbourhood or research different examples of microclimates or ecosystems.

- Does the area meet the basic survival requirements for bees; food, water and shelter?
- How would these differ in extreme climates?
- Do bees and other animals native to these areas need special adaptations to live there? For example, compare alpine or desert bees to urban bee populations.

3. BEES AT HOME

Bees are often categorized based on whether or not they exhibit complex or organized social behavior. Social comes from a word that means 'friend' or 'partner'. Social bees must live and work together in a community, while solitary bees are independent throughout the majority of their lifecycle.

There are varying degrees of social behavior. Honey bees, bumble bees and a few other species are referred to as being eusocial, or truly social, and exhibit four key types of social behavior, including;

- Adults who live in groups
- Cooperative care of young
- Division of labour, particularly reproduction
- Overlap of generations

Some bee species are considered to be semi-social and may nest in aggregations, with sisters or in communal nest structures.

The vast majority of bee species are considered solitary. All females can reproduce, and create and provision their own nests. Males can forage for themselves and spend most of their time seeking out female mates.

Most solitary bees are only active as adults for a few weeks at a time. During this time females will mate, seek out a nesting site and stock the nest with pollen and nectar. Females will lay up to 30 eggs (depending on the species) each within their own cell. Their offspring remain in the nest, often over winter, before emerging again in the spring.

Opportunities for Inquiry:

Explore the pros and cons of social vs solitary behavior.
- Which is more efficient in gathering food? How are resources divided?
- What sort of organization is required? How is nest defense managed?
- Design a game or activity that helps explore these concepts, with teams of 'social' or 'solitary' students.

Did you know?

Did you know? Wood-nesting females will lay female eggs at the back of the nest to protect them from predators, ensuring that there are reproductive females the following spring.

3.1 Members of the Hive

The division of labour in social colonies formed by honey bees and bumble bees has, over time, led to specific adaptations of each of the members depending on their gender and role. Each colony is a family that consists of three types of bees each with their own physiological variations: a reproductive female, the queen; infertile daughters, the workers; and the male drones.

3.1.1 Honey Bee Colonies

The queen is the largest bee and the only female capable of reproducing. She has a larger thorax and an elongated abdomen where she stores all the eggs she will have over her lifetime. The queen's compound eyes are small because she spends most of her life inside the dark hive and only leaves to mate or swarm to another hive. The queen can lay up to 2,000 eggs per day, which averages out to one egg every 45 seconds! Her lifespan ranges from two to five years.

Male bees are called drones and they are produced from unfertilized eggs. The queen will begin to lay drone eggs in late spring or early summer once the colony has recovered from its low winter population. The primary role of the drones is to mate with queens from neighbouring colonies. Drones are larger than the worker bees and are excellent fliers with especially large eyes to help them track queen

3. BEES AT HOME

bees on their nuptial flight. Drone bees do not forage for themselves, nor do they participate in hive chores, and their lack of stinger prevents them from being able to defend themselves or the hive.

The average drone lifespan is about eight weeks. When the weather cools and the nectar flow and pollen count decreases, the drones are forced out of the colony. This ensures that hive honey stores are available for the queen and workers over winter.

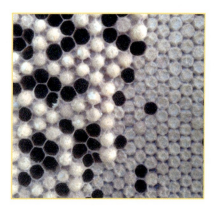

Did you know?

Drones are significantly larger than the worker bees. Consequently the queen lays their eggs in larger comb cells than the worker bees. Drone cells are identified by their puffy appearance. The adjacent photo shows drone brood on the left, compared with worker brood.

Opportunities for Inquiry:

Drones are called haploid organisms because they develop from an unfertilized egg containing a single set of chromosomes rather than a pair of chromosomes (diploid), as in worker bees (or humans). This is rather uncommon in animals and more frequently seen in the plant world.

- Explore how reproduction differs between haploid and diploid organisms. How does this relate to the production of seedless fruits or crop potatoes?

Worker bees make up the majority of the hive population, numbering in the tens of thousands and are the most commonly encountered honey bees in gardens and parks. The workers are all female and are the smallest members of the colony. The worker bee's life is divided into two parts: the hive period and the field period. Each period lasts between two to three weeks. The worker bees born in the fall can live for a few months over winter due to their decreased activity.

Newly emerged worker bees start hive chores right way, acting as cleaners for the hive and helping to keep brood warm.

After a few days, young worker bees become nurses and nannies to larvae, feeding them royal jelly, pollen and nectar. Some of the workers may also become part of the queen's retinue, grooming and feeding her.

Once bees reach about ten days old, glands in their abdomen start to produce wax which they use to construct the cells that make up the hive structure. Around this age workers may also start to help with transfer of nectar from foragers to cells.

3. BEES AT HOME

At around three weeks, older workers will start to take practice flights and guard the hive from intruders. Once they've perfected their flying, they will take on foraging duties, gathering pollen, nectar, propolis and water. The individual honey bees (including drones and queens) cannot survive for very long away from the other bees in the colony and will always return to their hive in poor weather or when the sun sets.

Did You Know?

On a calm sunny day, a worker bee may visit as many as 2,000 flowers!

Though there is a general sequence of tasks for worker bees depending on their age, they will perform any of the tasks required to ensure normal functioning of the colony. The expression 'busy as a bee' must come from all the work that they do to keep their hive healthy!

Opportunities for Inquiry:

- How does the organizational structure and roles in a hive compare to different political or economic systems you learn about in Social Studies?
- What about in a home or business? Review sections on Communication and Swarming in exploring how the colony makes decisions.

3.2 The Birds and the Bees

Bees, like butterflies, go through complete metamorphosis, a term that comes from a word that means 'change'. There are four distinct stages; egg, larva, pupa and adult. The season and duration of this process varies between species and is related to the social behavior of the bee.

3.2.1 Solitary Bees

Females build nests with individual cells for each egg. She first creates a small ball of bee bread, a mixture pollen and nectar, onto which she lays an egg. When the larva hatches out of the egg it will feed on the bread, gaining energy and fattening up. The larva then enters the pupa stage, where it starts to take on the physiological features of an adult bee. Most solitary bees will enter a stage of winter dormancy between the pupa and adult stage before emerging in the spring as a fully formed adult bee.

Did You Know?

Many solitary bees are only active for a few weeks every spring or summer. Bee enthusiasts may use the date of observation to help identify certain species.

3.2.2 Social Bees

Social bees move through the same stages of metamorphosis as solitary bees. However, the lifecycle of the colony depends on whether they are annual or perennial.

Bumble Bees:

Bumble bees are considered annual nesters because the reigning queen, workers and males die each fall. Only queens born that summer will survive through the winter to start new colonies the following spring.

3. BEES AT HOME

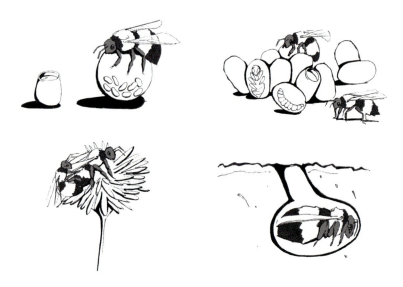

In the spring, new bumble bee queens emerge from hibernation and search for a nesting site. The very large bumble bees you may observe in your neighbourhood in early spring are usually queens. Bumble bees generally nest underground, typically in old rodent tunnels. They can also be found in dense dried grass or in hollows of trees. In urban areas bumble bee nests are sometimes found in sheds, roof soffits, under decks, or under sidewalk pavers.

Once she has found a cozy spot, she will build a wax pod and fill it with pollen. A second pod will be filled with a supply of nectar. She will then lay a few eggs on top of the bee bread and close the pod. The eggs must be kept warm, so the queen will sit on the pod, much like a chicken roosting on her eggs! As her offspring go through metamorphosis, she will mold the pod into individual wax cells around each larva.

The queen feeds off her stored nectar, making occasional trips to top it up, until the first generation of workers hatch about a month later. These worker bees will then take over all foraging duties and will help with the building of pods. This allows the queen to focus on laying eggs and caring for the brood.

Towards the end of the season, the queen will produce males and new fertile queens. Once they are mature, the males will leave the nest in search of mates. Young queens will also leave the nest to search for mates, but usually return each evening. Female bumble bees typically only mate with one male. As in the spring, in late summer you may observe the larger queens flying and foraging. As you develop your knowledge and observational skills about bees, you will enjoy noticing more and more about the bees that live in your habitat.

Mating bumble bees

The mated queens will spend the rest of the season foraging for nectar and pollen, building up fat stores for winter. As winter approaches, they will search for a cozy place to hibernate until spring.

Honey Bees:

The honey bee queen lays eggs in the bottom of a wax cell in the brood chamber area of a hive. Each egg is about the size of a comma. The brood refers to the eggs, larvae and pupae stages of bee development. All the brood needs are food, warmth and time to grow.

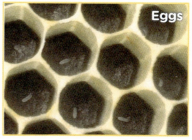
Eggs

Nurse bees keep the hive's brood chamber at 36 degrees Celsius to incubate the eggs. If it is too hot, they collect water droplets and fan the air with their wings to cool the air. If it is too cold, they cluster together to generate body heat.

Larvae

A worker bee egg hatches after three days, becoming a larva. The nurse bees make nutrient-rich royal jelly from glands on their heads and mix it with honey and pollen to feed to the larvae for the first three days.

3. BEES AT HOME

Following this, a larva is fed exclusively honey and pollen called bee bread for another six days. During this period the larva molts four times; shedding their skin and increasing in size.

At day eight, the larva has extended to the full length of its cell. At day nine, the larva spins a silk cocoon around itself and molts for the last time. The nurse bees then seal the top of the cell with wax to protect the bee in its pupa stage. Pupae do not eat, instead, they use energy from the fat and tissue they stored up when they were in the larval stage.

At around 21 days, the bee has reached the adult stage and will have to chew away at the capping on her brood cell before she can crawl out. Initially her hair will appear slicked back and light in color and her steps uncertain. Drones develop in a similar manner, though they take a little longer, about 24 days in total.

The development of a queen bee is a special process. When the workers want to create a queen, they select a regular worker egg and instead of feeding it royal jelly for three days, it is fed exclusively royal jelly for the full eight days prior to cell capping. This diet allows for the proper development of the reproductive system and other physiological features of a queen.

Honey bee larvae

Queen pupa

Bees are born

Queen cup larvae

Queen cell

About a week or two after she emerges as an adult, the queen will take mating flight, one of only two times she'll leave the hive. On her flight, she'll seek out 'drone zones' where males congregate in hopes of finding a queen. These areas are located in mid-air, sometimes over a kilometer high. When the queen nears the drone zone, the males will sense her pheromones and begin to pursue her. The queen will mate with around a dozen drones before returning to her hive. The sperm stored in her large abdomen will allow her to produce fertilized eggs for the rest of her life. The drones do not survive the ritual as their reproductive organs are torn from their bodies after mating is complete.

> **Opportunities for Inquiry:**
>
> Explore the different ways to mathematically or visually represent the different stages of metamorphosis and the time each type of bee spends in each stage.
>
> - How does this differ from other insects, or incomplete metamorphosis?

3.2.3 Swarming

Honey bee colonies are considered superorganisms because there are two types of reproduction in the colony; the creation of individual members of the hive and the duplication of the colony, as a whole, known as swarming.

When a colony has a large brood population and there is no more room in the hive, the queen bee releases a pheromone telling the hive that it is time to prepare to swarm.

The worker bees get ready to start the new hive by constructing some special elongated wax cells called queen cups in which they begin to raise new queens. These cells resemble a peanut shell in size and shape. At this point, the old queen stops laying eggs and she is kept away from the queen cups to protect the new queens. The nurse bees also feed her less to make flying easier when it is time to swarm.

3. BEES AT HOME

The queen then leaves the colony taking half of the workers (mainly older, forager bees) to find a new home. The swarm of bees is loud and resembles a dark, swiftly moving cloud. Though they can appear intimidating, they are extremely docile as they no longer have a hive to defend.

> **Opportunities for Inquiry:**
>
> Honey bee colonies travel en masse when swarming. There are other examples in nature of animals moving as a large group; starling murmurations, schools of fish, herds of elephants, human migration, and more! Investigate these and other examples of animals moving in large groups from place to place.
> - What are the reasons for their migrations?
> - What are the patterns? Using arts-based methods, how might you design words, movements, or visual mediums to depict and share your learnings about these travelling groups?

The queen will seek out a nearby resting spot, accompanied by her workers, often in a tree or other sheltered location off the ground. While she waits, scout bees will seek out a location for the new hive and report back to the colony on the best location. The entire swarm will then move into the new hive. The swarm can last for a couple hours to more than a day, depending on weather and the success of the scouts.

Back at the original hive, when the first new queen emerges, she will destroy any other queens preparing to hatch. After a week or two, when she is mature, she'll take her mating flight and begin rebuilding the colony to full population. A single colony will have become two. This is one way to ensure the survival of the species, as some colonies do not survive.

3.3 Hive Products

Nearly all bees gather and store nectar and pollen, though the amounts are so little that they're not worth the effort for most predators, including humans. The large, perennial colonies formed by honey bees make them a much more appealing focus. The variety and quantity of products produced by honey bees has attracted humans for millennia, who have used these items for nourishment as well as for medicinal, cosmetic and cleaning purposes.

3.3.1 Honey

Honey is made by bees converting the nectar collected from flowers through the processes of digestion, regurgitation and evaporation. When the nectar is eaten, it goes into its honey crop, a first stomach where special enzymes start to convert the nectar to honey. Some of the nectar goes into the honey bee's second stomach to feed itself.

When the bee returns to the hive, she transfers the nectar to other workers who store it in wax cells. At this point, there is still a high content of water in the honey, so the worker bees must then flap their wings to heat the air so the water will evaporate.

Once it reaches the proper humidity, the bees seal the cell with a wax cap. Beekeepers know that a frame of honey is ready for harvest when at least a third of the honey cells on it are capped.

> **Opportunities for Inquiry:**
>
> The transformation of nectar to honey is a form of food preservation.
> - What are the different methods that humans use to preserve food?
> - Why is it important? How is it like, or unlike, the creation of honey?

3. BEES AT HOME

Honey-making is a labour-intensive process. The average honey bee worker makes only 1/12th of a teaspoon of honey in her lifetime. The workers in a colony must visit nearly two million flowers to make just one pound of honey. Though this seems like an incredible amount of work, but depending where in the world the beehive is located, a colony can produce over 100lbs of surplus honey in a season. Some large colonies in these locations could produce up to 500lbs in a single season.

Honey is the main source of carbohydrates for honey bees. It consists mainly of water and sugar, glucose and fructose, but also has small amounts of vitamins and minerals. The exact components vary depending on the flower from which the nectar was gathered and this can influence taste, colour, smell, ratio of glucose to fructose content and speed of granulation.

Honey has other uses as well. It is antibacterial, antifungal and antiviral, which contribute to its almost infinite shelf-life. It has been used historically to help heal burns and wounds, to reduce joint swelling, and to soothe and disinfect a sore throat.

Opportunities for Inquiry:

Explore the different colours, smells, tastes and textures of honey. For example, compare clover honey to buckwheat and to comb to creamed to liquid. Some honeys are very mild tasting (clover or dandelion), while others have strong hints of bitter, or possible lingering after-tastes (chestnut).

- How can you design a system for recording your observations? Which would be best to use in a recipe for honey lemonade, and why? What about other recipes?

3.3.2 Pollen

Pollen is a highly nutritious food eaten by many insects and is vital for bees as a protein source during brood-rearing. Like honey, pollen is unique to the plant it comes from and contains a specific array of nutrients. In large successful hives, pollen can be collected by a beekeeper and used as a health supplement.

Did You Know?

A honey bee can carry up to 75,000 pollen grains on her body.

3.3.3 Propolis

Also known as bee glue, propolis is a sticky substance that bees use to help provide stability to their hive (like concrete) or to seal up cracks or holes. To make propolis, bees collect tree resin and combine it with pollen, nectar, water and enzymes from their mouths. This ensures the hive is waterproof and windproof and also helps protect the hive from natural enemies such as ants, wasps and mice.

Propolis also has antibacterial and antifungal properties which can help protect the health of the colony. For example, if the bees destroy an intruder that is too large to remove from the hive (ex. mouse), they will use propolis to 'mummify' it so the bacteria from the dead rodent will not harm the colony. The antibacterial properties of propolis made it a useful medicinal product throughout human history. People would use it as a wound treatment, to sooth dental issues and to treat other oral maladies.

3. BEES AT HOME

3.3.4 Royal Jelly

Royal jelly is a nutrient-rich substance produced by glands in the head of the worker bee. This substance is fed to all larvae for the first three days of their development mixed with honey and pollen. Queen bees are fed royal jelly throughout their larval stage and again as adults. The jelly contains vitellogenin which boosts the queen bee's immune system, reduces stress and also helps slow down aging throughout her body.

Royal jelly is also used by humans medicinally for a wide variety of ailments and as an immune booster. It is very difficult to harvest large quantities so it is a rather expensive product.

3.3.5 Beeswax

At around the time a worker bee is ten days old, wax glands located on her abdomen begin to produce liquid wax. As the wax is secreted it solidifies into delicate plates which are chewed by the bees to make them malleable. The workers use the wax to create the hexagonal cells that form the structure of the hive. The cells are built from top to bottom, hanging from a top support (wood, tree branch, etc.). Each sheet of wax has cells on either side, angled slightly above horizontal to prevent honey from dripping out. Bees store honey, pollen and brood in the wax cells.

> ## Opportunities for Inquiry:
>
> Comb in a honey bee hive is constructed out of repeating hexagonal shapes.
>
> - Investigate why honey bees build this way. Inquire into other shapes found in nature and human architecture.
> - What are the 2D and 3D forms?

When honey is harvested by the beekeeper, the excess comb wax can be gathered to be used in making products like candles, lipstick, artist crayons, shoe polish, floor polish, sealing wax, tree grafts and buffing wax for skis and surfboards.

Did you know?

Beeswax candles burn much slower than other candles because they have a high melting point.

3.4 Honey Bee Communication

A mature colony of honey bees can contain more than 60,000 workers! In order to keep everything running smoothly, a significant amount of communication has to occur between the hive members. The complexity of honey bee communication has fascinated scientists for decades and they are still discovering the subtle ways that honey bees communicate with their hive mates and the world around them.

3.4.1 The Waggle Dance

When a foraging bee finds a location with plentiful floral resources, she will return to the hive to share the details with her fellow workers...by dancing! Known as the waggle dance, the bee uses a set of movements to communicate distance and direction.

Did you know?

The dances usually happen inside the hive near the entrance or farther back in total darkness. Bees rely on their acute sense of smell, taste and touch to interpret the dance.

To communicate direction, the worker moves in a figure eight pattern, shaking her abdomen vigorously. The orientation of the figure eight corresponds to the location of the resource relative to the sun.

3. BEES AT HOME

If the forager bee waggles straight up towards the sun the flowers are located by flying straight towards the sun. If the forager bee waggles to the left or right the flowers can be found flying along the same orientation.

The speed of the waggle dance gives information on the distance of the flowers from the hive. If the food source is close the bee's abdomen waggles faster. The foraging bee also brings back the special scent of the flowers which gives additional information to the other foraging bees. As the nectar and pollen start to run out in that particular area, then fewer bees will do the dance and visit those flowers.

For resources within about 100 meters of the hive, workers will use a circular pattern which varies in intensity depending on the quality of the flowers. Workers who see the dance will travel in all directions from the hive, using scent as a guide.

Opportunities for Inquiry:

Bees are not the only animal to use the sun as their primary navigational tool.

- Explore how humans and other animals use celestial objects to find their way. How does this change around the globe?
- What are other forms of human navigation? How are we aided by tools? How do we record our findings and share them with others?

3.4.2 Pheromones

Honey bees have a keen sense of smell which plays a key role in how they complete hive tasks and communicate with fellow members of the colony. Like many animals, foraging bees will use their sense of smell to locate food, but it is their use of pheromones for communication which plays a significant role in colony life. Pheromones are body secretions that allow the bees to 'talk' to each other via smell.

- A hive's guard bees learn the pheromone hive scent of their nest mates. Bees carrying this smell are allowed into the hive. Bees without the familiar smell are considered potential robbers and the guards will prevent these bees from entering the hive.

- When a bee feels that the hive is under attack, by other insects, animals or clumsy beekeepers, she will emit a certain pheromone that warns other bees of the threat. In these situations, bees can sometimes be seen perched near the entrance with their abdomens in the air, using their wings to fan the pheromone towards other hive members to alert them of the danger.

- In addition to dancing, foraging bees exchange pheromones to assist each other in finding food and water.

- The queen bee produces pheromones to attract drones and to tell the hive when to swarm.

- When nurse bees touch the queen they pick up her unique pheromone. The retinue then passes the scent on to other bees through feeding or grooming. This is how the colony recognizes the queen and knows that she is healthy. As she ages or if she becomes ill, the queen's pheromone weakens. The decrease in pheromone signals to the rest of the hive that it is time to replace the queen.

Opportunities for Inquiry:

Apply the principles of the waggle dance to design a seek-and-find game or scavenger hunt using only 'dance' and movement for communication.

- What are the different ways that people or other animals communicate? How does communication differ if there is no shared language or one of the senses is gone?

4. BEES AND PEOPLE

4.1 Honey Bee Management

For thousands of years, humans have been intrigued by bees and their ready supply of fresh, sweet honey. The oldest evidence of humans gathering honey was found in Valencia, Spain, where cave paintings, dating back to 6000BC, depict women gathering honey from a bee hive. In all likelihood, the practice of gathering honey and other hive products began much earlier as pottery, dating around 7000BC, has been discovered throughout Eurasia with chemical evidence of beeswax.

The practice of beekeeping and maintaining apiaries is thought to have begun in Ancient Egypt, using hives made of mud and straw. Hieroglyphics, depicting the honey bee, originate around 3000BC, and shortly after, around 2500BC, sculptures depict people tending to hives and gathering and storing honey. Honey was an important part of Egyptian culture and economy. Recently, jars of still edible honey were discovered in an ancient Egyptian burial tomb and are thought to have been an offering to the gods. Honey and other hive products were a valuable trade item and ownership of colonies and swarms was protected by law, much like other kinds of livestock.

Beekeeping continued on, growing through Europe and Asia. In ancient Greece, honey was offered as gifts to the gods and to the spirits of the dead. Aristotle, and other authors wrote about bees and recorded beekeeping practices. In fact, the bees were so important that the Ancient Greeks put a symbol of the bee on one of their coins. When the first settlers arrived in North America, they brought the non-native honey bee with them.

Over the centuries, people have experimented with different types of hives. Different materials, like clay, straw and wood, were explored as well as physical orientation of components and access. Through history, beekeeping was limited by hive construction, which often made access to honey comb difficult. In most cases, harvesting honey meant damaging the hive to the point where the colony could not survive.

Did you know?

Honey bees are highly intelligent learners, and are sometimes used to detect un-exploded landmines, narcotics, and other dangerous substances. Bees trained to detect the target scent can be followed to the location of the dangerous substance or can indicate the presence of the substance on a sample of clothing or other material. Some bees are even fitted with microchips on their backs. As they fly, the electrostatic charge on their bodies attracts explosive chemicals and, when they return to the hive, a scan of the chip reveals which bees came into contact with the substance.

Opportunities for Inquiry:

- In what other ways do humans partner with animals?
  What skills do animals have that help people with these jobs?

It wasn't until the 19th century that beekeeping started taking technological leaps forward, when Reverend Lorenzo Langstroth invented the moveable frame hive. In this hive arrangement, stacked wood boxes each with rows of wooden frames, resembling a filing cabinet, allow beekeepers to remove combs of honey with very little disruption to the hive. The removable frames also allowed beekeepers to observe bee behavior at length and up close for the first time in history.

From this point forward, researchers and beekeepers made huge progress in understanding the lives of bees and the harvesting efficiencies launched modern commercial beekeeping as we know it today. In the present day, beekeeping occurs all over the world in range of scales, using different technology and beekeeping methods. Whether as large scale producers with thousands of hives, urban rooftop beekeepers or traditional wild honey hunters, humans still have a close relationship and fascination with honey bees.

4. BEES AND PEOPLE

4.2 Supporting Local Bees

Providing bees with a supportive habitat is one of the most important and significant contributors to bee survival, and something that you and your students can commit to in your own community. All over the world, communities, researchers and individuals are exploring ways to improve bee habitats and develop a better understanding of these important creatures. At the University of Bristol, researchers confirmed that urban areas can be just as important as farmland and natural areas for bee conservation. Community gardens in particular, with their high plant diversity, seem to be hot spots for bee diversity.

In Seattle, the Pollinator Pathway Project addresses habitat fragmentation by using private homes and boulevards to connect natural areas. A mile-long narrow strip of gardens and vegetation connects a small wooded park and Seattle University. The project not only provides additional habitat for bees and other pollinators, but asks urbanites to reevaluate how they design and transform the natural areas they inhabit and to consider the maintenance of ecological health as one of the foundations of urban planning.

Efforts to improve bee health and diversity have expanded to agricultural areas as well, where research has shown that preserving areas of natural habitat has been shown to increase local bee diversity and significantly improve pollination of adjacent crops.

It is not necessary to keep a hive or have acres of land to make an impact. Simple changes to one's own patch of green creates a stitch, that when replicated, can begin to weave nature back through communities. When creating a space for bees, it is most important to consider their main habitat needs; food, water, shelter and the absence of harmful chemicals.

4.2.1 Food

Providing food (flowers) for bees is perhaps one of the easiest and most effective ways to support one's local bee population. Not to mention the beauty of a colourful array of flowers! Bees require a steady source of pollen and nectar to feed them while they're active as adults and to provision their nests and offspring.

Different species of bees are active at different times of the year, so it is important to have a few plants blooming at all times, especially in spring and fall when many bees are either just emerging or are preparing for winter.

Consider the bee's shifted visual light spectrum. Yellow, purple, blue and white flowers are the most attractive to bees, though they will still visit some pink or red blooms. Flowers that are simple and single headed versus densely-petaled are generally easier for the bees to access. Larger bees, or those with long tongues are better equipped to gather nectar from more complicated flowers.

Bees like to make the most of each foraging trip, visiting as many flowers as they can in the shortest amount of time. For this reason, bees are more likely to visit large patches of blooms than single, sporadic flowers. Plant groupings at least one meter in diameter are ideal, but a collection of pots on a balcony or front step can have a similar effect. Where more space is available, blooming shrubs and trees can provide excellent forage for visiting bees.

Many plants that are considered garden 'weeds', such as dandelions, clover and nettle can provide an excellent source of nectar flow for the bees in early spring. In vegetable gardens, leaf or root plants can be allowed to flower (lettuce, radishes, beets etc.) to provide food for bees and to produce seeds for the following year.

Opportunities for Inquiry:

Research plants native to your area and plant seeds for a potted arrangement or garden.
- **Do any of the seeds require special treatment for germination?**
- **How would this benefit the seed and how would this be accomplished in nature? Examine vegetables or fruit to consider how a plant could feed animals and people in perpetuity through seed-saving.**

4. BEES AND PEOPLE

Native plant varieties can be especially beneficial to the local bee population. Because plants and bees evolved alongside each other, they are perfectly suited to one another. In fact, some solitary bees are known as specialists, feeding only on specific genera of plants. Providing these plants ensures that picky eaters aren't left hungry. Native plants can also be great for low-maintenance gardens because they are perennial and well-adapted to local climate conditions.

Bees also need a lot of water, so it is helpful to have a fresh source available. Bird baths, shallow dishes or small ponds will keep bees hydrated through the hot summer months. Providing bee watering dishes in your yard or community can provide an interesting place to observe bees and other pollinators.

Did you know?

It is important to add islands of sticks or rocks to shallow water sources. Since bees breathe through the side of their body, they can easily drown if they do not have a way to climb out of the water.

When creating a bee-friendly garden space, herbicides, pesticides, or other chemicals should be avoided. These can accumulate in dew, other standing water or on flowers and can make bees sick through contact or ingestion.

4.2.2 Nesting Sites

Suitable nesting sites are necessary for successful reproduction and are ideally located close to floral resources. The simplest approach is to determine whether existing nests are present and to protect these spaces from disruptive human activity.

Approximately 70% of bees build their nests in the ground. It can take some careful observation to determine where these nests are, but there are a few indicators to watch out for:

- Keep an eye out in sunny, sparsely planted areas. Look on stream banks, near the base of shrubs, in lawns and even in unused sand boxes or raised garden beds!

- Some ground nests will have a small mound of dirt near the entrance, similar to an ant tunnel. Watch these spots to see who emerges from the nest.

- Spend 15-30 minutes observing an area, keep an eye out for bees returning to a nest site with pollen or nesting materials.

Try to protect any confirmed sites or beneficial areas and keep in mind that observation can take some practice and may change from year to year.

Many different wood-nesting solitary bee species will happily take up residence in an artificial nest. These can be either bundles of hollow stems or holes drilled into wood.

- Nests should be placed in an open, east-facing location on or near a large landmark like a tree or side of a building.

- Nests should be protected from heavy winds and hot afternoon sun.

- Tunnels should be 10-16cm deep and open at only one end.

- A variety of tunnel diameters should be used to cater to a range of bees, ideally between 3/32-3/8th of an inch.

- Nests should be replaced every few years to prevent disease or pathogen build-up.

Hollow-stemmed shrubs, like raspberry or sumac can also be planted to provide natural nesting areas for local wood-nesting bees. Some species, like bumble bees, need a safe over-wintering sites. Leaving untidy garden spaces, with fallen leaves, small branches or compost can provide a safe and cozy space for these bees (and other beneficial insects) to spend the chilly winter months.

Opportunities for Inquiry:

Humans and other animals use a variety of materials to build their homes or nests.

- How are these the same, or different? How does the local environment influence what people or animals use to build homes?

5. GLOSSARY

Abdomen: The rear third of the bee's body, containing organs for digestion, reproduction and respiration.

Annual: A type of plant or bee nest/colony that lives for one year. Subsequent plants or nests are started from seed or a single bee respectively.

Antenna (pl. Antennae): The moveable, sensitive feelers on an insect's head used for taste, touch and smell.

Anther: Part of male plant structure, the area of the stamen that produces pollen.

Apiary (pl. Apiaries): A location where a colony or colonies of bees are kept. Apiculture is the science of honey bees and beekeeping.

Bee Bread: A bitter mixture of honey and pollen that is mixed by the bees in their stomachs and used as a food source for larval stage bees.

Beekeeper: A person who cares for a colony of honey bees, also is called an Apiarist.

Brood: All stages of immature bees: eggs, larvae and pupae.

Brood Chamber: Area of the honey bee hive that houses eggs, larvae and pupae. Some cells in this part of the hive may also hold pollen or honey that is used to feed the developing bees.

Cell: The single, hexagonal element that makes up the wax comb structure of a hive. Also describes a compartment of a bee nest which holds a single developing bee.

Chitin: The main component of the exoskeleton of a bee's body comprised of a polymer of glucose which can support a lot of weight with very little material.

Cocoon: A protective silk covering spun by larvae as they transition to the pupa stage.

Colony: A large, social group of bees containing one fertile queen bee along with drones and worker bees.

Comb: The wax structure made of hexagonal cells in which honey bees rear their young and store food.

Compound Eyes: The large eyes of a bee composed of many small lenses called ommatidia.

Corbicula: Stiff hairs on the legs of some bees used to carry moistened pollen. Also known as pollen baskets.

Drone: A male bee that is part of a social colony, produced from an unfertilized egg.

Entomologist: A scientist specializing in insects.

Exoskeleton: The hard, protective, exterior skeleton found frequently in the insect world. A bee's exoskeleton is composed of moveable plates of chitin.

Field period: The second part of a worker bee's life where it typically does most of its work outside the hive.

Forage: Either the act of gathering food or the food which is gathered.

Frame: A wooden rectangle that supports comb in a honey bee hive. Occasionally refers to a single panel of naturally formed comb.

Generalist: A bee that feeds on many different genera or species of plants.

Genus (Genera): A taxonomic rank that forms the first name in the binomial naming system. Groups species with shared characteristics.

Granulation: The natural solidification of glucose crystals in liquid honey. Can give honey a more opaque colour and coarser texture.

Habitat Fragmentation: The isolation of parts of a habitat by physical or ecological gaps. Can limit movement of species.

Hibernate: To enter a dormant state (usually seasonal) characterized by low metabolic rate, lower body temperature and slowed breathing.

(Egyptian) Hieroglyphics: A form of writing using pictures of objects to represent words or sounds.

5. GLOSSARY

Hive: The physical home of a colony of bees.

Hive Period: The first part of the honey bee's life where it typically spends most of its time working inside the hive.

Hive Scent: A scent produced by worker bees that is characteristic of their own colony and is recognized by the other members.

Honeydew: A sugary liquid secreted by aphids and other insects.

Honey Crop: The stomach-like organ of a worker bee that is connected by a valve to their digestive tract. Nectar stored here mixes with enzymes which initiate the transformation of nectar to honey.

Larva (pl. Larvae): The second stage of metamorphosis when the bee's segmented body is soft and worm-like. In this stage the bee consumes enough food to grow and fuel later development stages.

Lifecycle: Series of stages an organism passes through in its lifespan.

Maxilla: Portion of the tongue used for lapping. Located on the outside of the tongue structure.

Metamorphosis: The growth of an organism marked by distinct physical stages, sometimes with little similarity between them. Complete metamorphosis includes four stages: egg, larva, pupa and adult.

Mutualistic: A symbiotic relationship between two organisms in which both benefit.

Nectar: The sweet liquid secreted by flowers to attract pollinators.

Nuptial Flight: The flight a new, virgin queen bee takes to mate with drones from other colonies. Queens will typically only go on one mating flight.

Ocelli: The simple eyes bees use to orientate themselves towards the sun. (Ocelli is derived from the Latin word meaning "little eye.")

Oligolectic: A foraging preference in bees for certain types of plants, usually a specific genus.

Ommatidium (Ommatidia): The small hexagonal units that make up a bee's compound eye.

Ovule: Part of the female structures of a plant that hold its genetic material and becomes a seed after fertilization.

Palp: Part of the mouth structure that assists the sucking function of the straw.

Perennial: A type of plant or bee nest/colony that lives year after year. Either may have a period of dormancy or reduced activity between peak active or reproductive seasons.

Pheromone: A chemical odour made by an animal which serves as a signal to other individuals of the same species.

Pistil: The female reproductive part of a flower.

Pollen: A fine dust-like substance produced by plants containing the male genetic information. It is the source of protein for bees.

Pollen Basket: Stiff hairs on the hind legs some bees where they carry pollen. See corbicula.

Pollination: The transfer of pollen from one flower to another as part of the reproduction process.

Proboscis: A collection of structures that make up the tongue of the bee.

Propolis: A combination of plant resin, wax and saliva created by honey bees.

Pupa: The third, cocooned, stage of metamorphosis where the bee takes on the physical appearance of an adult. The bee does not eat during this stage.

Queen: The sole fertile female in a colony of social bees.

Retinue: Attendants to the honey bee queen. These workers feed, clean and care for the queen.

5. GLOSSARY

Royal Jelly: A milky yellow syrup secreted by worker bees from glands inside their heads. It contains protein, vitamins, fatty acids and minerals.

Scopae: Also called pollen brushes, these hairs are located on the hind legs or abdomen of some genera of bees. Dry pollen is stuffed into the dense hairs for transportation.

Simple Eyes: The three smaller eyes located in a triangular shape on top of the bee's forehead in-between the compound eyes. They sense patterns and intensity of light and dark.

Social: An behavioural structure used by some bees. Many bees live in a colony and share the task of raising their young. Behaviour can range from semi-social to truly social.

Solitary: A behavioural structure in which a female independently builds her own nest and raises her own young.

Specialist: A foraging preference in bees for certain types of plants, usually a specific genus.

Stamen: The male reproductive part of a flower.

Stigma: The sticky part of the female reproductive structure of the flower used for capturing pollen.

Swarm: The half of a honey bee colony that leaves to form a new colony. It is the reproduction of the superorganism that is the honey bee colony.

Tarsal (pl. Tarsi): Claws at the end of the bee's leg used for clasping onto rougher surfaces.

Thorax: The middle section of the bee's body that contains the flight muscles, wings and legs.

Taxonomic: Ranking system of biological organisms according to common characteristics.

Ultraviolet: Electromagnetic radiation with a wavelength shorter than that of visible (to humans) light.

Vitellogenin: A precursor to egg yolk protein that provides nutrients for egg-laying. A key ingredient in royal jelly.

Waggle Dance: A form of communication used by worker bees to indicate the location of floral resources.

Worker: An infertile female bee in a social colony. Participate in care of brood and hive/nest.

6. REFERENCES

Balch, T., Quitmeyer, A. (2011, February 2). The Waggle Dance of the Honeybee. Retrieved from https://www.youtube.com/watch?v=bFDGPgXtK-U

Bumblebee.org (2017, December 8). Bumblebee Behaviour 1,2,3, male. Retrieved from http://www.bumblebee.org/foraging.htm

Bumblebee.org (2017, December 8). Bumblebee Tongue and Mouthparts. Retrieved from http://www.bumblebee.org/bodyTongue.htm

Burlew, R. (2016, April 19). When Will a Newly-Emerged Queen Begin to Lay? Retrieved from https://honeybeesuite.com/when-will-newly-hatched-queen-begin-lay/

Collison, C. (2016, February 22). A Closer Look: Sound Generation and Hearing. Retrieved from http://www.beeculture.com/a-closer-look-sound-generation-and-hearing/

Collison, C. (2015, October 23). A Closer Look: Tarsal Glands / Footprint Pheromone. Retrieved from http://www.beeculture.com/a-closer-look-tarsal-glands-footprint-pheromone/

Department of Systematic Biology (2017, December 8). The Most Incredible Insects. Retrieved from https://www.si.edu/Encyclopedia_SI/nmnh/buginfo/incredbugs.htm

The Guardian (2010, October 24). Bees' Tiny Brains Beat Computers, Study Finds. Retrieved from https://www.theguardian.com/world/2010/oct/24/bees-route-finding-problems

Halter, R. (2011, August 26). The Incomparable Honeybee & the Economics of Pollination. Retrieved from https://books.google.ca/

Hive and Honey Apiary (2017, December 8). Fascinating Facts About the Honey Bee Brain. Retrieved from http://www.hiveandhoneyapiary.com/2015/08/12/fascinating-facts-about-the-honey-bee-brain/

Honey bee (2017, December 8). Queen Retinue. Retrieved from http://honeybee.drawwing.org/book/queen-retinue

Kienlen, A. (2016, February 23). Wild Bees Can Boost Your Yields. Retrieved from https://www.albertafarmexpress.ca/2016/02/23/wild-bees-can-boost-your-yields/

Kritsky, G. (2017). Beekeeping From Antiquity Through the Middle Ages. Retrieved from http://www.annualreviews.org/doi/pdf/10.1146/annurev-ento-031616-035115

Lau, C.W. (2012, December). Ancient Chinese Apiculture. Retrieved from http://labs.biology.ucsd.edu/nieh/papers/Lau2012.pdf

National Geographic (2015, November 23). Honey in the Pyramids. Retrieved from http://www.nationalgeographic.com.au/history/honey-in-the-pyramids.aspx

PerfectBee (2017, December 8). The Anatomy of Bees. Retrieved from https://www.perfectbee.com/learn-about-bees/the-science-of-bees/the-anatomy-of-bees/

Peters, A. (2013, November 26). The Queen Will See You Now: How Bees' Sense of Smell Might Soon Diagnose Disease. Retrieved from https://www.fastcompany.com/3022123/the-queen-will-see-you-now-how-bees-sense-of-smell-might-soon-diagnose-disease

Pollinator.ca (2017, December 8). Wind Pollination (Anemophily). Retrieved from http://www.pollinator.ca/bestpractices/wind_pollination.html

Prigg, M. (2013, April, 26). The Croatian 'Bomb-Bees' That Can Sniff Out Landmines From Three Miles Away. Retrieved from http://www.dailymail.co.uk/sciencetech/article-2315198/The-bomb-bees-sniff-landmines-THREE-MILES-away.html

Riddle S. (2016, May 20). How Bees See and Why it Matters. Retrieved from http://www.beeculture.com/bees-see-matters/

Scientific American (2017, December 8). Why Do Bees Buzz? Retrieved from https://www.scientificamerican.com/article/why-do-bees-buzz/

Scott, E. (2013, February 23). Bee Keepers' Day – Apis Through the Looking Glass. Retrieved from https://adventuresinbeeland.com/2013/02/24/bee-keepers-day-apis-through-the-looking-glass/

Sheen, J.P. (2002). Chitin. Retrieved from http://www.encyclopedia.com/science-and-technology/biochemistry/biochemistry/chitin

Traynor, J. (2002, June). How Far Do Bees Fly? One Mile, Two, Seven? And Why? Retrieved from http://beesource.com/point-of-view/joe-traynor/how-far-do-bees-fly-one-mile-two-seven-and-why/

University of Exeter (2016, February 4). Bee Virus Spread is Human Made, Driven By European Honeybee Populations. Retrieved from https://www.sciencedaily.com/releases/2016/02/160204150617.htm

von Frisch, K. (2014, September 3). Dance Language of the Honey Bee. Retrieved from http://articles.extension.org/pages/26930/dance-language-of-the-honey-bee

WebMD (2017, December 8). Propolis. Retrieved from https://www webmd.com/vitamins-supplements/ingredientmono-390-propolis.aspx?activeingredientid=390&

Yong, E. (2010, November 2). Bee-ware – Bees Use Warning Buzz to Refute the Waggle Dance. Retrieved from http://phenomena.nationalgeographic.com/2010/02/11/bee-ware-bees-use-warning-buzz-to-refute-the-waggle-dance/

Manufactured by Amazon.ca
Bolton, ON